Royal
Wedding Album

November 1948 was not a particularly auspicious time to be born. Britain was in the severest grip of post-War austerity – rations were short, the economy was weak and the outlook was gloomy indeed. The loss of the Indian Empire in 1947 bewildered many who could not reconcile the fact with the hard-won victory of the Allies in the War, while the first faltering moves towards a Socialist-inspired Welfare State lacked the flair to give the British people confidence for the future.

In the three years since the end of the War, the country had had little to celebrate – yet the ordinary citizen was quick to take what opportunities there were. In November 1947 the heiress to the Throne, 21 year old Princess Elizabeth, married her third cousin, Philip Mountbatten, a naval officer whose father was Prince Andrew of Greece, and the country erupted in a universal demonstration of spontaneous loyalty and affection at the sight of a handsome young couple about to go forward together into the uncertain future. The following April saw the Silver Wedding celebrations of King George VI and Queen Elizabeth, who by their show of steadfastness, courage and oneness with their people during the six years of war, had raised themselves and the Crown to a level of love and popularity exceeding

(1) Princess Elizabeth and her sailor husband, Lieutenant Philip Mountbatten, at Buckingham Palace after their wedding at Westminster Abbey on 20th November 1947. Despite the prevailing austerity, the marriage took place amid customary royal splendour, as the richness of the Princess's long lace-trained wedding-dress suggests (5). Surrounding the royal couple on the balcony (4) are King George VI, Princess Margaret, Queen Elizabeth and the eighty-year-old Queen Mary. (2) Princess Margaret's wedding to Antony Armstrong-Jones thirteen years later was the most sumptuous royal occasion since the Coronation. (3) Princess Anne with Captain Mark Phillips, waving to enthusiastic crowds from the Palace balcony after being married in Westminster Abbey on 14th November 1973. (6) The Princess and her husband kneel at the High Altar after the solemnisation of their marriage. (7) A father's helping hand as Princess Anne is led up the aisle by Prince Philip. As the service

4

1

2

3

5

that which had so surprised King George V at his Silver Jubilee in 1935.

Now, in November 1948, neither the national difficulties nor the appallingly bitter weather could prevent this loyal nation from taking the closest interest in the imminent birth of a direct heir to the Throne, as Princess Elizabeth, with her husband the Duke of Edinburgh, awaited her first confinement, at Buckingham Palace. For a while it seemed that the event would never happen – the public had been expecting news at the end of October – but when on 13 November the head of the team of gynaecologists took up residence in the Palace, the crowds knew that the time could not be far away, and they were right.

begins, she stands (8) with her bridegroom and his best man before the Archbishop of Canterbury, Dr Michael Ramsey. (10) Accent on youth: Princess Anne and Captain Mark Phillips with the only page, Prince Edward, and the only bridesmaid, Lady Sarah Armstrong-Jones, in this official photograph taken at Buckingham Palace by Norman Parkinson. (9) Royal wedding with a difference: Prince Michael of Kent emerges from the Town Hall of Vienna after a civil ceremony of marriage to the Roman Catholic Baroness Marie-Christine von Reibnitz in June 1978.

6

7

8

9

10

The following evening it all happened. It was not a quick or easy birth – the Princess had to be anaesthetised for a forceps delivery – but when it was all over, with the birth of a boy at precisely 9.14 pm, there was rejoicing both inside the Palace and beyond its walls.

The Duke was the first to know that the birth had taken place and that he was now the father of a Prince. When the Princess awoke, her husband was there beside her with the news and a large bouquet of roses and carnations. The King and Queen made themselves responsible for directing hundreds of telegrams to relatives and foreign statesmen, whilst the crowd milling anxiously outside the Palace was at last informed of the event – first by a policeman in the forecourt, and then by an official bulletin, at 10.15 pm.

How they cheered and sang and speculated on that bleak and dark November evening! It is not often that

(1) The Queen Mother sees the wedding of the first of her grandchildren to be married: she rides with Prince Charles back to Buckingham Palace after Princess Anne's wedding. (2) Princess Anne and her husband do homage to the Queen as they leave the chancel after the registers have been signed. (3) Important little people: Lady Sarah Armstrong-Jones and Prince Edward as bridesmaid and page. (4) Part of the procession heading back towards Buckingham Palace after the wedding. (5) Princess Anne on the arm of Captain Phillips as, followed by Prince Edward and Lady Sarah, they proceed towards the West Door of the Abbey and out into the streets of London.

1

2

3

4

5

him. His daily life in the royal nursery, his outings in one or other of the royal parks, his journeys to Sandringham and Balmoral and Windsor, his clothes, his toys, his nannies and his meals – even his bath-times became topics of daily interest to Press and people alike in Britain and beyond. All eagerly awaited the latest photographs of him and a whole range of newspapers and magazines found new life in the business of keeping their readers minutely informed of the little Prince's progress.

Progress there was, but it came in a form that few of us would appreciate. By the same star which occasioned the adulation surrounding his birth, he was deprived of the normal upbringing by which every parent would wish to benefit a child. Prince Charles' father served in

e Palace cares to suppress loyal enthusiasm but, after o hours of constant chanting and wild celebrations, a essage pleading for silence had to be issued as the rincess needed to rest and could not do so because of e noise. After the second attempt, the crowd gradually spersed and went on its weary but joyful way.

Despite the more official celebrations that followed – e flags, the telegrams, the presents and the poetry – thing was known of the new Prince until his Christening a month later at Buckingham Palace. Here he was med Charles Philip Arthur George by the Archbishop Canterbury; the baby was dressed in a long robe of niton lace which had been used for such occasions ce the baptism of Queen Victoria's eldest child in 40. Amongst his Godparents were his two great-andmothers, Queen Mary and the Marchioness of ilford Haven, his grandfather, King George VI, and a eat-great-uncle, King Haakon VII of Norway. The ficial photographs were issued on that day and for the st time Britain could take stock of its future King.

From that day, Prince Charles of Edinburgh became e of the most famous babies in the world, and the rld, it seemed, clamoured for every latest detail of 8

the Mediterranean for the first three years of his so
life and was rarely at home. Princess Elizabeth had
deputise increasingly for her ailing father and, as
pressure of official duties mounted, so the young Pri
saw less and less of his parents. Living in Claren
House – just down the road from his doting gra
parents in Buckingham Palace – helped, of course,
did the arrival of a sister and companion, Princess An
in August 1950, but a world in which a child sees nann
as parents and parents comparatively infrequently m
have seemed baffling indeed. Even when his fatl
returned from the Mediterranean in July 1951, stabil
failed to materialise: his parents were off on a tour
Canada three months later, and his grandfather the Ki
underwent operations for suspected cancer. In Janu:
1952, the Princess and her husband left home again fo
Commonwealth tour which the King himself was too
to undertake. After only a week, the King was dead a
Prince Charles' parents hastened back home as Que
and Consort. Little did he know it, but at the age
barely three, the shy and charming boy born to be Ki
himself was now only a step from the Throne, and mo
drastic changes were in store.

The education of the eldest sons of British sovereig
was never considered a potential problem before t
First World War: the general definition of education w
narrow and with royalty it was even narrower. Suited
a limited education might have been to a future monar
(whose role in public life was likely to be far less tangil
than it has proved to be in the 20th Century) the ne
Queen and her forward-looking husband were quick
evaluate the rapid changes in society's structure a
mores and to react accordingly when it came to choosi
an education for young Prince Charles. At first the
was no outward sign of the transformation and t
Prince took lessons on his own at Buckingham Pala
under the active eye of his tutor, Miss Catheri
Peebles. In 1956, his day's lessons were interrupted
that he could spend the afternoons attending Hill Hou
School in Knightsbridge for games, as part of a gen
and tactful move towards being introduced to t
necessity of meeting, relating to and learning with oth
boys. He became a full time day boy at Hill House a
spent 1957 there, gaining recognition for his love
history, his extensive reading and painting abilities, a
his aptitude for cricket and wrestling. Unfortunately, l
mathematics was – and remains – a comparatively we:
point.

Prince Charles was subsequently sent as a boarder
Cheam School in Hampshire. Like Hill House, it was
school attended by his father before him and it w
noted for a decidedly more liberal mode of educati
than was likely to be found at other public schools. F
the Prince it was at first a cruel blow – still reserved a

Prince Charles' early life was, like that of most royal children this century, punctuated by the annual pattern of Easter holidays at Windsor, Summer at Balmoral and Christmas and New Year at Sandringham. Usually the Royal Family travelled as a large group

by train: (1, 2 and 4) the Queen leaves King's Cross for Balmoral with the young Princes, Andrew and Edward, and (3) Princess Margaret greets Prince Andrew as she and her children, Viscount Linley and Lady Sarah Armstrong-Jones, wait to join the

*royal train for Sandringham at Liverpool Street Station.
(6) Prince Charles as Colonel-in-Chief of the Royal Regiment of Wales: he wears the Garter Star, having been installed as a Knight of the Garter in June 1968. (5) The simple and beautiful ceremony of*

Prince Charles' Investiture as Prince of Wales at Caernarfon Castle on 1st July 1969. The proceedings took place in Welsh and English, and after the investiture proper, the Prince rose to deliver a speech in both languages. (7) An official portrait

of the newly invested Prince of Wales, who carries the regalia the Principality and wears the Prince of Wales' crown which h been specially made for the occasion. His ermine and velve robe is worn over regimental uniform.

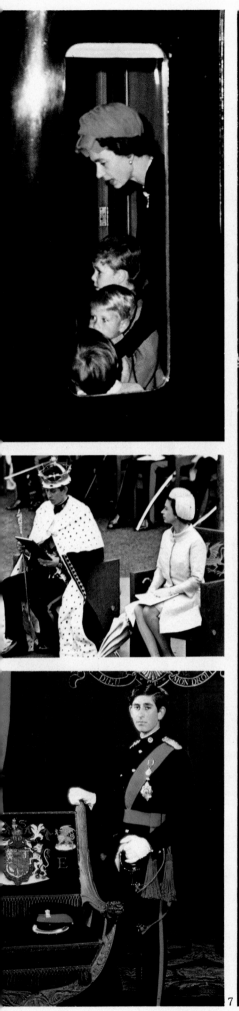

unsure of himself, he was now without governess or parents at hand, sharing a dormitory with other boys, utterly dejected at the prospect of having to mix with his more outgoing colleagues, and feeling for the first time what he later called a "ghastly, inexorable sense" of being a boy apart from others.

That feeling had, of course, been nourished for years – journeys in chauffeur-driven cars and special trains; curious or cheering onlookers; pressmen anxious for public and private pictures; hushed formality at home; special clothes for special occasions as he witnessed his mother take part in colourful, revered ceremonial in London, Windsor, Scotland . . . all this had over those first ten years made its mark. Now he was thrown into a different and unfamiliar maelstrom in which some boys kept away from him because of who he was, and others latched on to him for the same reason. He, himself, found great difficulty in assessing the sort of life he wanted, needed, or was expected to lead.

Things were made no easier when, in June 1958, the Queen made public her intention to create him Prince of Wales. Enthusiastic though the reception was, both at Cardiff Arms Park, where the announcement was made, and at Cheam, where it was heard on television, it caused Prince Charles acute embarrassment and only slowed his painful reconciliation with the fact that, as the heir to a unique throne, he had to learn to live as normal a life as possible.

Although he may never have felt entirely settled at Cheam – and his school reports reflected a continuing uneasiness – signs of assurance started to appear. His love of outdoor activities – swimming and horseriding – began to manifest itself as he grew into early adolescence: he grew more interested and better informed about the events in his own private life – Badminton, Braemar, Trooping the Colour – which he had hitherto regarded as mere ritual. In 1960, there was the birth of a younger brother, Prince Andrew, together with the happy family celebration of the wedding of his aunt, Princess Margaret, to Mr Anthony Armstrong-Jones. He matured psychologically in this period to such an extent that his bearing at important occasions and private outings alike commanded public approbation for its sheer self-confidence. By 1962, when the next stage of his education began, he was a wholly different being from the timorous and retiring boy at Cheam.

In that year he followed his father's footsteps again – this time to Gordonstoun, a public school in the north of Scotland, founded by another liberal educationalist Kurt Hahn, a man ahead of his time. The more spartan

Balmoral is the Queen's summer holiday home, and it is here that the Royal Family is seen at its most relaxed and informal. (1) The Queen and Prince Philip are joined by their three sons on the lawns in front of the Castle in 1979. (2) Later, the family group is completed by Princess Anne and her son Peter, in the nearby woods. (3) No royal outing would be complete without a contingent of corgis! (4) Prince Charles celebrated his twenty-fourth birthday in November 1972 with this delightful picture showing him with his cousin Lady Sarah Armstrong-Jones at Balmoral. (5) Prince Charles with the Queen and Prince Andrew watching Princess Anne compete in the Montreal Olympics in 1976. (6) Prince Charles' 30th birthday portrait, taken in the grounds of Balmoral: with him is his golden labrador, Harvey.

1

2

3

4

5

(1) The Queen makes her entry into St Paul's Cathedral for her Silver Jubilee service on 7th June 1977. Accompanying her is Prince Philip, who turns for a brief word with Prince Charles. Behind them is the Master of the Queen's Horse, the Duke of Beaufort. (5) The balcony scene after the Queen's Silver Jubilee service as she and Prince Philip acknowledge the cheers from below: with them are Captain Mark Phillips, the late Earl Mountbatten of Burma, Prince Andrew, Prince Edward and the Prince of Wales. (2) Prince Charles accompanies his grandmother, Queen Elizabeth the Queen Mother on the way to St Paul's for a thanksgiving service for her eightieth birthday. (3) On the Palace balcony afterwards, the Queen Mother waves appreciatively to the crowds of wellwishers. With her are her two daughters, her son-in-law Prince Philip, and her six grandchildren. (4) Later, inside Buckingham Palace, the Queen Mother makes a fuss of one of the corgis as the royal group poses for photographs to commemorate the great day.

traditions of the school–a cold shower and pre-breakfast run every morning, and lending a hand with the daily chores, were well publicised and tended to obscure the comprehensive curriculum which spread far beyond academic subjects taught at other secondary schools, public and state, at that time. In addition to sport there was military-style training; in addition to painting there was music-making and the creative arts; and in addition to learning at the desk there was activity and action in the fullest sense. The five years he spent there were certainly the most fulfilled of his life to date – including as they did the achievement of five 'O' levels and 2 'A' levels, the title role in the school play, 'Macbeth', graduation to Head Boy (or Guardian) by 1966, and a two-term 'sabbatical' at Geelong Grammar School in Australia–an introduction to the breezy, forthright and exciting ways of scholars and citizens alike in that part of the Commonwealth, where he accepted the appellation 'Pommie Bastard' in the very best part!

There followed, in 1967, an unusual episode in Prince Charles' educational career when it was decided that– notwithstanding his average academic achievements– he should go to Trinity College, Cambridge. It was in a sense a negation of much that had been planned for him because it took him out of a world of some realism, where he was forced to mix, into a much more sheltered environment where he could have retired into his shell. The decision not to make him part of the normal three-year degree intake, but to devise an individual course

6　　　　　　　　　　　　　　7

(6) Prince Charles escorts his sister Princess Anne from the House of Lords after the State Opening of Parliament in 1976: he attended in full dress naval uniform, while she wore formal evening dress and tiara. (7) Happy at Windsor: Prince Charles leaving St George's Chapel after the service of the Most Noble Order of the Garter.

specially for him seemed doubly inappropriate at the time. As it was, Prince Charles found himself at last free to pursue his own interests, both academically – he chose history, archaeology and anthropology – and socially. He became an active member of the Dryden Dramatic Society, and famous for his roles as dustmen, weather forecasters, vicars and lechers.

He studied the cello, developed his now ever-growing love of classical music in all its forms, and increased his knowledge of archaeology. At the end of it all, in 1970, he emerged with a BA Degree in History – class 2. This was by no means a discreditable outcome of the first royal experiment in the wider form of education, particularly since in the middle of his time at Cambridge his studies had been seriously interrupted by his Investiture as Prince of Wales.

Scheduled to take place at Caernarfon in July 1969, the Investiture was designed to be a repeat performance, with the necessary modifications, of the grand ceremony of 1911 when Prince Charles' uncle (later King Edward VIII) became the first Prince of Wales to be publicly installed and presented to his people since the son of Edward I in the 14th Century. There was enormous excitement over the forthcoming pageantry, as well as more than a touch of bitterness from those Welshmen who resented an event celebrating the implied domination of Wales by England. That bitterness manifested itself by bombs and bomb threats, local acts of sabotage and noisy demonstrations against Prince Charles himself during some of his visits to his Principality. But he quickly became accustomed to them and learned to keep a sense of proportion sadly lacking in his adversaries. When asked how he felt as the Investiture Day approached, he said, 'As long as I don't get covered too much in egg and tomato, I shall be all right.'

By that time, however, the public relations department of Buckingham Palace had done its work in the most efficient manner. The Prince had been sent on a four-month course to learn, amongst other things, the Welsh language at the University of Wales in Aberystwyth. He had been involved in several embryo schemes concerning the welfare of the Welsh, had visited many of Wales' major towns and climbed the mother of her mountains, Snowdon. On top of it all came the television film 'Royal Family' – a 2½ hour master-

3   4

5

1   2

(1) Prince Charles taking a morning dip during a visit to Australia, and (6) – a common feature of his visits down-under jogging along the beach after his swim. (2) Cooling off after a game of polo – one of his favourite sports – at Windsor. (3) The Prince about to mount his horse for another game of polo, and (5) offering his pony a well-deserved titbit after a match. (7) He enjoys stiff competition on the field and (8) strides out with confidence as he kits himself up for the next game. (10) Member of

the side: Prince Charles with both teams before the start of a polo match. (4) In 1979 Prince Charles took part in the triathlon event at the Royal Windsor Horse Show. (9) Skiing is another favourite sport: the Prince at Klosters, in Switzerland. (11) Up...Prince Charles masters the art of wind-surfing on the Solent during Cowes Week. (12) Over...The wind drops and he is sent off balance. (13) Out...After a thorough ducking, he clambers out of the sea and tries again.

6   7

9

10

12

13

piece of entertainment and information to satisfy the steadily growing public interest in this unique event, culled from the extensive public and private life of the Queen and her family.

When the great day came, the loyalty of the Welsh was almost entirely assured. They gathered thickly along the route from Caernarfon station to the Castle as the Prince, with his parents, sister, aunt and grandmother, arrived, and stayed to welcome him as the Queen presented him three times at the gates of the Castle after the ceremony. For Prince Charles, this simple act of dedication to Wales and homage to his mother and Queen set him on the road of public duty in Wales, and of a long and happy relationship with his future subjects in Britain and the Commonwealth. It was also very much his coming of age; an entry into manhood. As he bore himself with a curious but apt mixture of modesty and confidence, his people – and surely he himself – realised that his life of service had begun.

The word 'service' was no mere expression of convenience. The Prince of Wales, already an eligible bachelor with an assured future and only a moral obligation to exert himself, was not content with a passive acceptance of his role. At Cambridge he had already learned to fly and it was the RAF that he joined soon after his graduation. At the Training College at Cranwell in Lincolnshire, he completed a course of instruction in flying jet aircraft and a successful parachute jump. 'It's easy when you're pushed' he said later. In 1971 he was awarded his wings, just like his father in 1953. Later in 1971 he joined the Navy, entering Dartmouth like so many previous members of the House of Windsor, but as a sub-lieutenant rather than as a midshipman. He served on the guided missile destroyer, HMS *Norfolk*, and by way of the frigates *Minerva* and *Jupiter*, was put in charge of the mine-sweeper, HMS *Bronington*. In the meantime, he underwent an assault course at the Royal Naval Training Centre at Lympstone and was posted to the Royal Naval Air Station at Yeovilton, where he completed 15 hours solo flying and sufficient ground training to make him the best officer on his course, and ready to join a Naval Air Squadron on HMS *Hermes*. When he left the Royal Navy in 1976, he was better qualified and much more experienced than any Prince of Wales completing service in the armed forces of his time.

These achievements were all the more impressive since his public duties outside the services became increasingly burdensome during that time. Although he did not emulate the previous Prince of Wales as a lone, roving ambassador to all parts of the Commonwealth

(1) The sailor Prince, in full naval uniform, attends the re-dedication ceremony for his old ship, HMS Bronington, at Chatham.
(2 and 3) In November 1976, as Lieutenant the Prince of Wales, Prince Charles captained the minesweeper as she took part (5) in a counter-mine exercise in the Firth of Forth in Scotland, and showed himself to be conscientious (11) and relaxed (10). Again in full dress naval uniform (4) Prince Charles listens to the *speeches of welcome on his arrival in Wellington for a 12-day visit to New Zealand in March 1981.*
(7) Prince Charles about to take off in a Wessex 5 helicopter which he piloted during an exercise at RAF Yeovilton. (6) The helicopter in full flight, complete with Royal Standard. (8) The Prince in training gear on manoeuvres, and (9) on more formal duty, inspecting a battalion after the presentation of Colours.

1

2

3

4

(1) Smiling, but tight-lipped, Lady Diana Spencer faces a daunting phalanx of photographers and newsmen who followed her almost every day from her flat in West London to the Pimlico kindergarten where she worked. These were the difficult days of Autumn 1980 when speculation about her relationship with Prince Charles was at its height. (3 and 4) "Shy Di" can't resist a quick peep to see if the photographer is still there. Despite her good-humoured acceptance of public and press interest, many people, including her mother who made a protest to the Press, wondered whether this did not amount to harassment, or at least, unfair treatment of a 19-year-old girl. (5) Lady Diana looks just a little annoyed with all the attention, but at no time did her tact and patience break, and her admirable self-control in such impossible circumstances was highly commended. (6 and 7) More games of hide-and-seek as Lady Diana returns to her flat, and a clear indication that she will

and the world, he began to undertake extensive and varied journeys abroad, usually with other members of his family, as soon as he was out of college. 1970 was a particularly busy year: in addition to attending the Independence celebrations in Fiji, he visited Canada and New Zealand with the Queen and Prince Philip, and the USA with Princess Anne, as guests of President Nixon. He also attended the memorial service for President de Gaulle in Paris that November on behalf of the Queen. In 1971 he spent several weeks in East Africa on tour with Princess Anne (whose prime interest in the visit was as President of the Save the Children Fund) where he met President Kenyatta of Kenya, the former Mau Mau leader. In 1972 he joined his parents during their State Visit to France, and was able to be present as the Queen and her uncle, the Duke of Windsor, met for the last time. In 1973, he represented the Queen in the Bahamas, which became independent that year.

In 1975 he was despatched to Papua New Guinea for another independence ceremony, and attended the coronation of his good friend King Birendra of Nepal. Part of a crowded Jubilee Year was taken up by an ex-

6   7

answer no questions nor pose for photographs. After the announcement of her engagement, Lady Diana became more open and relaxed: (2) she graciously accepts a daffodil from Cheltenham schoolboy Nicholas Hardy, who was then accorded the privilege of kissing "the hand of my future Queen." This picture was taken at Cheltenham on the day the Privy Council in London gave its consent to the forthcoming marriage.

tensive tour of West Africa in February and March: there was another trip to Canada during which he attended the Calgary Stampede, and late in the year an exciting, spirited tour of a dozen or so major cities in the United States.

1978 brought a lengthy tour of Latin American countries, 1979 another visit to Australia, and it seemed totally appropriate that he should be delegated to represent the Queen when the troublesome and delicate question of Rhodesia was finally settled and the new republic of Zimbabwe was born.

Since then he had undertaken a momentous tour of India and a further visit to Australasia, during both of which he experienced the warmth of eager and welcoming thousands as well as the hostile chants and derisory jeers of minorities with axes to grind and frustrations to vent – which Prince Charles took in his now measured and flexible stride.

All of which suggests that the Prince is a serious man, thoroughly duty-bound by upbringing, environment and character, with neither time for recreation nor aptitude for fun. Nothing can be further from the truth: the fact is that his official activities are so efficiently arranged and undertaken at such a cracking pace, that he is able to make time for his many leisure activities. Polo has been such a longstanding favourite pastime that, having achieved a consistent excellence at the game (though he has only once played for England) it would be foolhardy to allow his interest and abilities to wane at the behest of official duties. He is also a devotee of skiing – a sport he first took up amid a barrage of Pressmen in the mid 1960's – and manages to tuck a few days away at Klosters, a fashionable Swiss ski resort, between engagements on the Continent in January or February each year. Unlike his cousin, the Duchess of Gloucester, he has yet to break a leg! More recently, he has converted his love of sailing into a flair for windsurfing and can be seen annually trying his (none too successful) hand in the Solent during Cowes Week.

Even more recently he has developed his horseman-ship to the point where he is now qualified for steeple-chasing under National Hunt rules. Unfortunately, his success at this trickiest of equestrian sports has been extremely limited and his career has been pitted with ill luck. His first race was probably his best – at Plumpton in March 1980 he rode Long Wharf in a thirteen-horse charity race, in which he left too much light between himself and the eventual winner and had to be content with second place. The promise this showed was never fulfilled: he came last out of four in his following race, on Sea Swell, and on the point of retrieving his future on Allibar (originally the Queen Mother's horse) he was robbed of success when the horse suddenly dropped dead after returning with Prince Charles from the training gallops, in February 1981. It was a blow which failed to discourage him, although in his two succeeding races he was unseated and thrown from his new mount, Good Prospect.

But there are always the recognised country pursuits – hunting, shooting and fishing – at which Prince Charles has done satisfactorily enough. Despite protests about blood sports, he does hunt, but not regularly, and spends much of his summer holiday fishing with his friend, Lord Tryon, in Iceland. Indeed, it was here in August 1979 that he heard, with revulsion and grief, of the assassination of his favourite uncle, Lord Mount-batten.

1

2

4

5

(1) Lady Diana in her element: holding two of her charges at the Young England kindergarten in Pimlico in September 1980.
(4) The building in Kensington where she shared a flat with friends: after her engagement, she went to live with the Queen Mother at Clarence House. (5 and 6) Engagement Day – 24th February 1981 – and Prince

Charles and his fiancée pose for photographs on the front lawns of Buckingham Palace: their oneness is symbolised (3) as the Prince of Wales' signet ring is seen with Lady Diana's ring of diamonds and sapphire. (2) Lady Diana in happy mood as she visits the Gloucestershire Constabulary at Cheltenham in March 1981.

3

In addition to all these activities, Prince Charles s finds time for, and pleasure in, classical music – part ularly operatic performances – reading (and writi prefaces to many books on subjects close to his hea and painting.

Heir to the Throne, royal ambassador, ex-member the forces, sportsman, well-travelled and widely re: the Prince of Wales could not but be the target of doze of attempts by Press and public alike to marry him c The opportunities for speculation on his choice of a w have been numerous and all such opportunities ha been taken. One of the earliest arose when he was r yet 21, when Prince Charles was the guest of Govern General Dorman of Malta, whose daughter, Sibel acted as his hostess and spent many days enjoying s and sea with him. There were girls from the locality Sandringham with whom he corresponded whilst aw and shared interests with whilst at home. There was t fresh, lively Davina Sheffield with whom he w frequently seen at equestrian events. At one stage, a: for some considerable time, the speculation turned favour of Lady Jane Wellesley, a childhood friend, a: daughter of the Duke of Wellington, who himself wa: close acquaintance of the Queen and Prince Phil: Despite repeated Palace statements which denied romance, their continuing friendship, and more part: ularly, the Royal Family's visit to the Wellingtons' hon for a Game Fair around this time fired the public intere almost into a frenzy.

But the public reckoned without Prince Charle extreme caution and deliberation. Aware from the tin of his Investiture of the need to marry, if at all, a pers he could be sure would fulfil her eventual duties Queen Consort, and whom he could not only love, b love and live with for life, he spent the 1970's almost a: in search of the perfect girl. Princess Caroline

Although Lady Diana had already been seen with Prince Charles at Covent Garden on 3rd March 1981, the first official function at which she accompanied him was on 9th March, almost a fortnight after their engagement. The occasion was a recital at *Goldsmiths' Hall, London in aid of the Royal Opera House Development Appeal, and a vast crowd of spectators had gathered well in advance of the royal arrival to catch a glimpse of the future Princess of Wales. She arrived in a revealing, almost daring, black* *taffeta evening dress which provoked a veritable firework display from the flash-bulbs of the waiting photographers, and caused a sensation in the Press the following day. Throughout it all Lady Diana looked and acted in the most natural and charming* *manner, as these pictures show. Another royal guest at the recital was Princess Grace of Monaco, seen (opposite page, centre) in earnest conversation with Lady Diana in the ante-room at Goldsmiths' Hall where drinks were served before the* *performance. Princess Grace, herself a commoner at the time c her engagement to Prince Rain: in 1956, no doubt impressed her upon Lady Diana as an example of how the royal style can be accomplished without compromising one's personality.*

Monaco was mooted as a candidate, but a meeting between her and the Prince in 1977 led no further. Princess Marie-Astrid of Luxembourg was said at one stage to be on the point of being engaged to Prince Charles, but, certainly for reasons of their differing religions, and possibly for other, more private reasons, the event did not materialise. There were other daughters of foreigners – Lucia Santa Cruz, a Chilean, and Laura Jo Watkins, his American guide during his 1977 tour – and there were more English girls, such as Jane Ward, whose friendship was brought to an abrupt end after she related details of it to the Press, and Anna Wallace, who took exception to Prince Charles' allegedly cavalier treatment of her at an official function and never saw him again.

Oddly enough, it was his friendship with Lady Sarah Spencer which resurrected the public feeling that the Prince might after all marry an English Rose, which he had long before suggested he might. He spent a skiing holiday with her at Klosters, and she shared his interest in polo. But it was during one of their meetings, at her home, that he began to take an interest in her younger sister, Lady Diana. She was then a 'splendid 16-year-old', as Prince Charles put it, and would have a couple of years to wait before the chance invitation to spend a short time at Balmoral Castle during a visit to her sister, who was about to give birth to her first child. When a photographer spotted the Prince and Lady Diana together, in that summer of 1980, the romance became very public property. After a further six months' courtship, in the most difficult and most unconducive circumstances, in the glare of the world's press, and under the scrutiny of almost every eye in the country, the once shy schoolboy who, in spite of himself, became the mature, intelligent and personable 21st Prince of Wales, made his choice and was accepted. Lady Diana Spencer would become the next Princess of Wales and future Queen of England.

The news of that choice became public some three weeks after it had been made. For although Lady Diana had entertained no qualms about accepting her suitor as her husband-to-be, Prince Charles insisted that, during her forthcoming short holiday in Australia, she should reflect on the disadvantages as well as the privileges of the relentlessly public life into which she would be marrying.

After her return, she confidently reaffirmed the absence of any doubts whatsoever, and so, after a celebratory dinner party at Windsor Castle, attended by the entire Royal Family, 24th February 1981 was selected as the day on which the public announcement should be made.

It came in a form common to almost all such announcements, though with that touch of archaic quaintness which sets the royal proclamation apart from all others: 'It is with the greatest pleasure that the Queen and the Duke of Edinburgh announce the betrothal of their beloved son, the Prince of Wales, to Lady Diana Spencer, daughter of the Earl Spencer and the Hon. Mrs Shand-Kydd'.

The first people to hear the news directly were those

attending an Investiture at Buckingham Palace – an unexpected bonus even for those fortunate or deserving enough to be there at all. But the Press, radio and television authorities, Parliament and Commonwealth leaders, were almost simultaneously informed, and as the news spread around the globe, the official telegrams of congratulation and good wishes began to pour into Buckingham Palace. Meanwhile, the public who, understandably enough, had for some weeks begun to lose interest in what appeared to be following the familiar pattern of an imaginary romance spun by the media, was taken mildly by surprise at this official confirmation that, at last, Prince Charles had wooed and won the hand of the most hotly tipped favourite of all.

Personal details of Prince Charles' girlfriends had rarely featured seriously and strongly in previous Press reports, and it was not really surprising that, despite earlier publicity, the British public knew comparatively little about its future Princess of Wales. It knew, because of that publicity the previous autumn, that she worked as a kindergarten teacher in Pimlico, and that she shared a flat in Knightsbridge/Kensington with three girl friends. It knew, vaguely, that her father, Earl Spencer, had been divorced from his first wife and had remarried a woman whom everyone had previously known as Raine, Lady Dartmouth. It knew, equally vaguely, that the frothy and eccentric Barbara Cartland and the missing Lord Lucan featured somewhere in the family tree. More than that was pretty well unappreciated by the man on the Clapham omnibus, the woman on the Tyneside Metro, or indeed anybody driving his or her vehicle up and down the motorways of Britain.

It was not long before that information arrived. The following morning's newspapers, full of freshly taken photographs of the happy couple on the front lawns of Buckingham Palace, were thick with particulars of Lady Diana and her family, sufficient in depth and width to stun an ox. The most significant factor – at least Debrett's thought so because they had researched it all several months before – was that she was certainly well enough connected. She and her Prince shared common ancestors in Henry VII and James II: additionally Lady Diana had the dubious distinction of tracing descent from Charles II, via no fewer than five of his mistresses. Around half a dozen major ducal lines, and a number of illustrious aristocratic families further peppered her ancestry.

More recently Lady Diana's family had strengthened its connections with the British monarchy through a veritable catalogue of honorary posts in the royal household, and of royal patronage at the font and at the altar. Two of her grandmothers were (and one still is) attached to the household of Queen Elizabeth the Queen Mother, a brother-in-law became Assistant Private Secretary to

(1) Lady Diana Spencer smiles gamely as she prepares to exchange her bouquet for a spade with which to help plant a tree to commemorate her visit with Prince Charles to open the Mountbatten Exhibition at Broadlands in May 1981. (2, 3 and 4) Afterwards she embarked on a walkabout to meet some of the spectators. (5) Lady Diana with Prince Charles at the end of their visit. (6) Lady Diana looks about her as she waits for Prince Charles to take his turn in the tree-planting ceremony. (7 and 8) Lady Diana at home with young and old alike.

1

2

3

4

5

6

7

8

Lady Diana experienced her first taste of royal ceremonial in June 1981. Prince Charles had already taken the salute at the second rehearsal of the Trooping the Colour ceremony, and the following week he accompanied the Queen and Prince Philip (1 and 6) to the ceremony proper. This was the occasion when a youth in the crowd fired six blank shots at the Queen as she passed close by. The tension of the next few minutes is clearly registered on Prince Charles' features (5) but later, on the balcony of Buckingham Palace (3), the royal composure is recovered as, for the first time, Lady Diana appeared – with Prince Charles, Lord Nicholas Windsor, Prince Philip, the Queen, Mr Angus Ogilvy, Lady Davina Windsor, the Duchess of Kent, the Earl of Ulster, Princess Alexandra, Prince Andrew, the Duke of Kent and the Queen Mother. Three days later, Lady Diana was present at St George's Chapel Windsor to witness the service for the installation of new Knights of the Garter. This unique annual occasion – the oldest, and arguably the most colourful ceremony of its kind in Europe – took place in glorious weather, which gave the thousands of onlookers the best

the Queen, and her father had been Master of the Royal Household in the 1950's; in addition both the Queen, the Queen Mother and Queen Mary were Godmothers to various members of the Spencer clan, and royalty attended their weddings. So, like the Queen Mother before her, Lady Diana Spencer was, from that point of view, a fitting bride for a future king.

The prestige of her background was not matched, however, by her upbringing, which had been comparatively modest and rather sad. Born, appropriately enough, only half a mile from Sandringham House – at Park House, which her father tenanted from the Queen – she was only six years of age, and an unsuspecting pupil at a King's Lynn nursery, when her mother vanished overnight from the house. It transpired that she had left her husband and children for Mr Peter Shand-Kydd, whom she later married. Lord Spencer, whose wedding at Westminster Abbey had been the social highlight of 1954 and whose marriage was without doubt steadily declining, found himself left, without warning, in sole charge of his three daughters and an infant son.

To relieve the domestic burden, the daughters were sent off to private boarding schools. Lady Diana, bemused and uncomprehending, was transferred from her day nursery to a prep. school, Riddlesworth Hall, near

6   7

opportunity to see the foot procession from the Castle to the Chapel, and the carriage procession back again. Prince Charles (7) was among the members of the Order taking part, and Lady Diana – who will one day, presumably, become a Lady of the Garter – watched with evident enjoyment from the top of the Chapel steps (4) as her future husband entered his carriage after the service, for the drive back to the Castle.

Diss. Her termly and occasional visits to a home which lacked the touch of a caring mother were strange and perplexing, and the psychological effects of the later necessity to spend part of her holidays at home with her father, and part at a totally unfamiliar house with her mother, must have been enormous in a child so young. To say nothing of the harrowing experience of life with 130 other schoolchildren during the weeks, two years later, when her parents' divorce case became almost celebrated for the grit which both parties displayed in contesting it.

It may have gone a long way towards explaining why Lady Diana's progress at school was slow and unspectacular, despite her natural charm and kindness and the persistence of her sheer effort to excel. Eventually, and without having excelled, she moved from Riddlesworth to West Heath School, a girls' public school in Surrey, which she left in 1977 without so much as an 'O' level, or indeed any real idea of what she wanted to be or do in future life. She spent a few desultory weeks at a finishing school in Switzerland, which she quitted on her own sudden impulse – knowing, however uncertain she might have been as to her immediate or ultimate future, that the tailor-made education for the daughters of gentlefolk was not for her.

Once back in Britain, she began to reorientate herself and eventually joined a small team of teachers at the Young England kindergarten in Pimlico. And it was there, in the middle of September 1980, that she consented to being photographed with her charges, and virtually became public property for the first time.

'The situation', said Queen Mary in 1910, after a few months as consort of the new King, George V, 'is no bed of roses'. The present Queen Mother no doubt experienced the same feeling in the early weeks of her husband's reign, coming as it did hard on the heels of King Edward VIII's abdication; and perhaps the Queen herself found the first few months of her reign fraught with difficulties she had never had cause to envisage. Certainly Lady Diana who, in a television interview on the day of her engagement (and with a confidence which, in a 19-year-old girl, had possibly been equalled only by Queen Victoria herself) proclaimed that she never had any doubts about what she was doing, must have been seriously assailed by misgivings within a matter of weeks.

For almost immediately the disadvantages which Prince Charles had pointed out to her began to emerge. Though neither the royal couple nor anyone else could reasonably have expected a totally unqualified cheer of approval from Parliament, a keen sense of hurt followed the desperately unfriendly and well publicised words of that seasoned anti-Monarchist, Willie Hamilton MP who, not without substantial support, berated the Palace, Government, local authorities, media and public alike – either expressly or by implication, for causing, permitting or encouraging enormous sums of public money to be spent on what was essentially a private occasion – particularly in the light of the considerable private wealth of the families concerned.

There existed, too, in those early days, a noticeable – if to some extent expected – antipathy against Lady Diana's 'step-grandmother', Barbara Cartland, the author of some 300 novels full of young, aristocratic and pure virgin love, which some found romantic and readable, and others found gushing and unrealistic. It was imagined that she might use this family occasion to

In May 1981, Lady Diana and Prince Charles visited Tetbury (1 and 2), not far from their future home in Gloucestershire. (3) Highgrove House, the imposing mansion where Prince Charles took his bride to live after their wedding: the Prince bought it after declining the gift of Chevening House in Kent. (4 and

5) Lady Diana's first attendance at a State banquet given by a foreign monarch; she arrives at Claridge's with Prince Charles to dine with King Khalid of Saudi-Arabia in June. (6) A serenely happy couple at Broadlands – the home of Prince Charles' favourite uncle, the late Earl Mountbatten – in May.

plug or justify some of her past utterings on the sanctity of marriage and the sheer exquisite romance of a pure young couple falling in love. In effect she hardly had the chance: an ill-concealed contempt, particularly in the gossip columns and other parts of the Press, burst into frenzied criticism when it was revealed that Miss Cartland had helped to arrange for British Airways to bring over parties of wealthy Americans to visit the newly-famous Spencers at Althorp Hall, the family seat in Northamptonshire, and take tea with them for an all-in sum of £900 a head.

Although the furore at this supposed 'cashing in' on the royal wedding died down when it was revealed that the tour had been arranged many months before the engagement was announced, the affair soured those early weeks – as indeed did the lesser matter of the allegations, the full veracity of which they denied, that the Spencers were now charging preposterous sums for photographers to take pictures of Althorp Hall and its contents. Though the Spencers remained untroubled, by the time the wedding invitations were out, Barbara Cartland had decided to quit. She declined an invitation from Lord Spencer's batch of 50, on the ostensible grounds that the occasion was essentially one for young people, and she in her eightieth year did not think it right to take up a place which might otherwise go to a younger member of the family. Later something nearer the real truth came out when she complained that she was 'sick to death' of the royal wedding – 'a frightful bore which everyone had spoiled by being "so horrid and bitchy"'.

There were other traumas to come, but for the present there was no getting away from the general and understandable admiration for Prince Charles and his fiancée as a thoroughly likeable couple. Interest abounded as to how Lady Diana, 12 years younger than the Prince, would conduct herself now that she was so firmly a part of the royal scene. Certainly her life had changed dramatically from the very day of the engagement. She had immediately left her West London flat and moved to Clarence House for the duration, under the protective and schooled eye of the Queen Mother. (Touchingly it was here that on her first full day she and Prince Charles spent the evening at an intimate dinner party with the Queen Mother and Lady Diana's grandmother Ruth, Lady Fermoy.) Lady Diana forsook, for all public purposes at least, her nippy little red Mini Metro for the sleek official Rolls-Royce in which her fiancé was so accustomed to ride; and she was now

One of the most recent of Prince Charles' many tours abroad was to India in November 1980, where for many of his engagements he was garlanded, and wore the vermilion daub symbolising the honoured guest (1 and 2). His clothes ranged from the formal (4) when he visited Mother Teresa's Sanctuary for Homeless Children, to the casual (7) whilst making a speech under this huge luxuriant canopy. Among his previous tours: America in 1977, when he sat in a moon buggy at the Houston Space Center (3); Papua New Guinea in 1975 for the independence celebrations (5); Australia – during his 1979 visit he wore this insect-resistant headgear (9); and South America in 1978, which included an energetic night out in Rio de Janiero (10 and 11). In 1981, Prince Charles revisited Australia and New Zealand, where he spent much of his time with children (8) and obligingly wore the flowers (6) and garlands (12) he received.

1

2

3

4

5

9

10

11

12

guarded by bodyguards and detectives as rigorously as any member of the Royal Family.

But throughout it all, she remained as natural and amiable as if nothing had changed a bit. Her public wave, as she now glided past crowds of curious well-wishers, was light and almost diffident, her general demeanour informal and affable. And when she stunned everybody by turning up at Goldsmiths' Hall for her first official function, wearing a more daringly low-cut dress than anyone could recollect as having been worn by any member of the Royal Family, any sense of outrage was tempered by the delightful charm and, in a strange sense, modesty with which she behaved.

On that occasion, she had, in addition to Prince Charles, an escort in the shape of Princess Grace of Monaco – herself a commoner before her marriage to Prince Rainier in 1956 – who calmed any nervousness Lady Diana may have felt by timely flurries of hen-talk as Prince Charles busied himself with the officials who were hosting the event. But as, at the end of this truly memorable evening, she passed with superlative grace the battery of whirring and flashing cameras into the royal car neither she, nor the vast crowds who saw her on that rainy evening, could have harboured any doubts that Lady Diana Spencer had indeed arrived.

By this early date, arrangements were already in hand for the wedding ceremony itself. Its date had been chosen as July 29th, slotted conveniently between the end of the Royal Family's 'summer term' of duties and engagements, and Cowes Week – the annual marine beano usually attended by Prince Philip, his three sons, Princess Alexandra, Mr Angus Ogilvy and their children, while the remainder of the Royal Family makes tracks for Balmoral or elsewhere.

It was to be a Wednesday, and the question hopefully arose as to whether the day would be declared a Bank Holiday, which in due course it was. Unfortunately schoolchildren did not in the event benefit, since the school term had ended by then, and several thousand holiday-making families whose annual vacation had long since been booked for that week lost out too. Even those who were counting on being at work that week could not be certain of their day off, since it transpired that a Bank Holiday automatically affected only those employed by banks or other financial institutions, or those who had contractual arrangements in that regard with their employers. It seemed in the fullness of time, however, that most large companies conceded the point in favour of their staff, subject to the exigencies of their

Royal Ascot in June saw Lady Diana Spencer accompanied by various members of the Royal Family on different days. On the first day she was driven down the racecourse in the customary way, with Prince Charles at her side, wearing an eye-catching hat with her smart striped outfit (5). The royal couple's departure after the racing was less ceremonial (6). Next day Princess Alexandra of Kent (1 and 4) escorted Lady Diana, who wore a simpler straw hat (3) in contrast to Princess Alexandra's slightly more flamboyant choice. On the third day, stripes were again in favour, whilst a plainish hat was set off by a large flower in the hatband (2). In June also, Prince Charles visited New York to attend a charity gala. Despite noisy demonstrations against the British presence in Northern Ireland, there were happier moments, such as this meeting with Mrs Nancy Reagan, wife of the President (7).

1

2

3

4

5

own particular financial situation. In the case of the Co-op, for instance, the closing of all its shops to allow a holiday for its 150,000 staff involved a prospective loss of £1½ million. But the Co-op agreed to the holiday, unlike the Glasgow firm of William Paton, lace-makers, who decided that commercial considerations had to come first, so that staff absenting themselves for the day would be liable to disciplinary action.

It was with some general surprise that the news was received of Prince Charles' decision to be married in St Paul's Cathedral rather than in Westminster Abbey. Almost every royal wedding since that in 1922 of the Princess Royal, the only daughter of King George V and Queen Mary, to the Earl of Harewood had been held at the Abbey, and although the possibility of a variation of venue in 1981 had not been totally discarded, the almost sanctified tradition which brought three generations of royal brides to Westminster had seemed immutable.

For Prince Charles there were thought to be other considerations. With his close family ties, he doubtless bore in mind that in recent years two particularly enjoyable occasions – his mother's Silver Jubilee and his grandmother's eightieth birthday – had been celebrated by thanksgiving services at St Paul's. He was as inevitably mindful too that, less than two years previously, it was to Westminster Abbey that he had come to mourn, with the bitter grief of an admiring great-nephew for an admirable great-uncle, the death of Earl Mountbatten of Burma, assassinated in August 1979 by members of the IRA. That sombre ceremony in the beautiful but severely Gothic Abbey may well have proved too memorable for the Prince to have chosen it for his own nuptials.

St Paul's had the additional advantages of light, architectural warmth and, most significantly of all,

11

12

Prince Charles' horse-racing career did not begin in earnest until 1980, although for many years he took part in the Royal Family's private morning gallop down the course at Royal Ascot (2). In March 1980, he rode Long Wharf (10) in a charity race at Plumpton, making a promising start (5) and just failing to finish first (6). He competed twice more in steeple-chases that year, riding Allibar, who unfortunately died in February 1981 after a training run. Prince Charles has since ridden Good Prospect but without great success: at Sandown (1) he was unseated as Queen Elizabeth the Queen Mother and Princess Margaret (7) watched with Lady Diana Spencer (12). At Cheltenham (3, 4, 8 and 9) Prince Charles looks confident enough at the three day March Festival, one of the most prestigious events in the National Hunt calendar.

space. It was reckoned that the building was capable
seating at least 500 more people than Westminst
Abbey, and although the wedding was an essential
private occasion, it was clear that the distincti
between the Royal Family's private and offici
connections could not be drawn sufficiently sharply
exclude large numbers of people from the necessity
being invited. 'It is not every day,' said Queen Victor
in 1858, 'that one marries the eldest daughter of th
Queen of England.' Given that that was said in
different context, a large seating capacity could h
justified in 1981 on the grounds that the marriage of
Prince of Wales was a similarly rare occurrence.

So St Paul's it was. Disappointed though the choi
may have been to the clergy and staff at Westminst
Abbey, it was not, on proper reflection, as momentous
decision as it at first seemed. It was, after all, only duri
the present century that the Westminster traditic
stretched back: none of Queen Victoria's many childre
nor indeed her grandchildren – save one – had marrie
there, the preference having been for priva
ceremonies at the royal palaces or, in the case
Princess Beatrice, the old Queen's youngest child,
small parish church on the Isle of Wight! Neverthele
the choice of St Paul's carried an historical significanc
in that the last Prince of Wales to have married there w
Prince Arthur, son of King Henry VII, almost fiv
hundred years before. That marriage, in the o
cathedral that stood before the Great Fire of 166
consumed it, was quickly doomed for both partners: th
Prince died within a matter of weeks, and his brid
Princess Catherine of Aragon was, after a dece
interval, married to the King's second son, who becam
Henry VIII. The history of that union is too well know
to be recorded here, but fortunately Prince Charles an
Lady Diana did not feel sufficiently superstitious
regard those historical misfortunes as in any wa
ominous for their own wedding.

Prince Charles made a further fundamental brea
with tradition in choosing to have, not a best man, bu
two 'supporters', whom he named as Prince Andre
and Prince Edward, his two younger brothers. Princ
Andrew, at 21 years of age the elder of the two, was
charge of the wedding ring, which was fashioned fro
what was left of a nugget of Welsh gold which had bee
used to make up the wedding rings of the Queen Mothe
the Queen, Princess Margaret and Princess Anne, an
which, once placed on the new Princess of Wales' finge
would sit beneath the £30,000 diamond and sapphi
engagement ring which Prince Charles had bought fo
her the previous February.

*Lady Diana Spencer's ordeal by
publicity in the days between her
engagement and her wedding was
not made easier by eager and
continuous interest in her fashion
sense, yet in that time she has
become noted for her independent
tastes and the distinctive character
of her clothes. Her first major
"trial" may well have been at Royal
Ascot in June, when, in the event,
she was compared favourably with
other royal ladies (1 and 2). More
recently, she accompanied Princ
Charles to the wedding of his
friend Nicholas Soames and M
Catherine Weatherall, in Londo
and for this occasion she wore a
striking light-weight red dress
with matching hat (3 and 6)
adding a new dimension to the
range of royal styles to which
Princess Margaret (4) and the
Queen Mother (5) have
contributed.*

For her part, Lady Diana helped to choose her brides-maids and pages: these included three members of the Queen's family – Lady Sarah Armstrong-Jones, the 17-year-old daughter of Princess Margaret, Lord Nicholas Windsor, the 11-year-old son of the Duke and Duchess of Kent, and India Hicks, the imaginatively named granddaughter of Earl Mountbatten, Viceroy of India in 1947. Then came Sarah Jane Gaselee, the daughter of Prince Charles' horse trainer, Clementine Hambro, a pupil at Lady Diana's kindergarten, Catherine Cameron and Edward van Cutsem, children of close friends of Prince Charles and Lady Diana.

At about the same time, it was announced that the designers of the bride's wedding dress would be the London firm of Emanuel – partnered by an avant-garde-looking couple, David and Liz Emanuel, who had been responsible for that much talked-about black gown which their esteemed customer had worn at Goldsmith's Hall. Speculation naturally persisted about the styling of the wedding dress, particularly when Liz Emanuel talked of 'fairy princesses' and the 'romantic' ideal. At a later date, rumour had it that no fewer than three different dresses had been designed as a precaution against premature leakage of information.

The Royal Wedding celebrations began in Hyde Park on the eve of the wedding day itself. At 10.15 on the night of 28th July, the Prince of Wales, watched by his family, 120 royal and distinguished guests and more than 500,000 people, lit a bonfire in Hyde Park – the first of 101 beacons to be set alight throughout the length and breadth of the country. Then began the most massive display of fireworks since the occasion in 1749 for which Handel wrote his Royal Fireworks music. In an almost continuous programme lasting over half an hour, the huge crowds and millions of television viewers were treated to a brilliantly colourful and noisy set piece which drew gasps of admiration from the enthralled spectators. The pièce de résistance was the world's largest Catherine Wheel, fixed to an enormous hoist. When lit, the Wheel spread its flame over a diameter of 100 feet. Throughout the programme, massed bands and choirs performed a complementary selection of music in the arena fronting the main display.

1

2

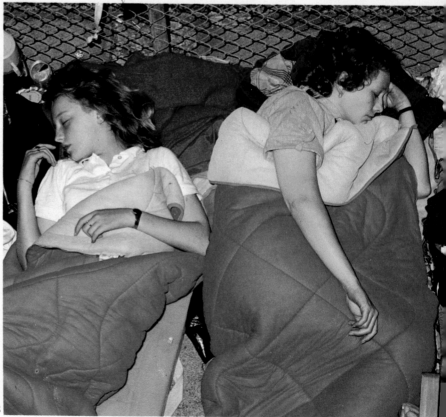

3

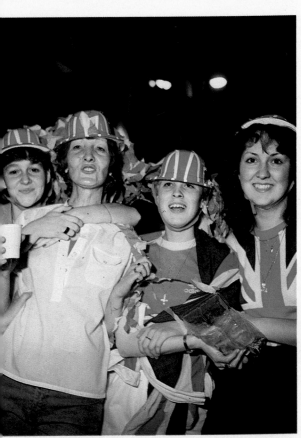

A full two days before the wedding, London began to team with tourists anxious to sample the atmosphere and see the processional route with all its bunting. The first campers positioned themselves outside St Paul's Cathedral and Buckingham Palace on the night of 27th July. Fortunately, the weather remained warm and dry, and despite the long hours of waiting, spirits were never wearied. Groups of patriotically dressed visitors (1, 4 and 6) revelled in the relaxed atmosphere and their boisterousness reflected the spirit of the occasion. Others found sleep an absolute necessity and endured considerable discomfort for up to

two nights on hard pavements (3). For everyone concerned, it was a time for proclaiming a degree of loyalty which at other times seemed hardly to exist. The Press abounded with pictures of the royal couple (7) and messages of good wishes were displayed on the front pages. Those without their flags and banners made do with a simple badge (5). Happily, at no time was there any serious crowd trouble and the huge contingent of 3,000 police were given an easy time. With instructions to get to know the crowds they were called upon to control, they were as pleasantly surprised to meet co-operation and good humour (2) amongst the people as the people were to find the police so relaxed.

One thing proved certain, however, and that was that the dress would be made of pure silk. This news brought widespread, if temporary, fame to thousands of Dorset silk-worms which were televised, photographed and reported on as they were being gathered from the mulberry bushes in May to be set to work producing the required silk at Lullingstone. The silk-worm farm there has been supplying silk for royal occasions since the Coronation of King George VI in 1937.

Since the wedding was to be a private, and not a State, occasion, the responsibility for the arrangements fell not to the Earl Marshal but to the Lord Chamberlain. There was an early hint of acrimony when the Earl Marshal, the Duke of Norfolk, discovered that his services were not required, but the rule stood, and Lord Maclean set to work. One of his first considerations concerned the massive royal procession which would thread its way along the Mall, past Trafalgar Square, up the Strand, Fleet Street and Ludgate Hill to St Paul's – and, of course, back again. Accommodation was required and found for a total of twenty-eight members of the Royal Family and sixteen other participants – the bride's parents, bridesmaids, supporters, and Household staff.

The issue was not made easier by the decision to anticipate the strong possibility that the traditional English summer would provide sufficient rain on the day to warrant the use of closed coaches. Mindful of the Coronation in 1953 when a sudden downpour doused the procession and spectators alike, and of the Silver Jubilee when, just as the Queen reached Buckingham Palace after returning from the Guildhall, the rain came down again (though it failed to disperse the million-strong crowd), the Palace decided that it was better to be safe than sorry, and that for senior members of the Royal Family the option of open or closed carriages should be available. Fortunately the stock of State transport at the Royal Mews was ample to meet the requirement of thirteen vehicles – ten to be used in fine weather, three of which were to be substituted for closed coaches if conditions turned inclement. The bride in any event travelled from Clarence House in the exquisite Glass Coach, in which the Queen, Princess Margaret, Princess Alexandra and Princess Anne had each been brought to their weddings.

Determining the form and content of the marriage service gave Prince Charles and Lady Diana the opportunity to illustrate their support for Church unity. While the Archbishop of Canterbury, Dr Robert Runcie, was to conduct the service, prayers were to be said by the Roman Catholic Archbishop of Westminster, the Moderator of the General Assembly of the Church of Scotland, and a member of the Anglican Community of the Resurrection, and the lesson would be read by Methodist Mr George Thomas, the Speaker of the House of Commons and a close friend of Prince Charles. This strong ecumenical element was warmly approved except by the most rabid Protestants who found voice in the Rev Ian Paisley: he announced that he would not be attending the service if the Archbishop of Westminster were to take part.

The Prince of Wales' love of classical music prompted

him to choose a fairly traditional selection of ceremonial music, including works by Handel, Jeremiah Clarke, Purcell and Orlando Gibbons, with modern composers being represented by Holst, Elgar, Parry and William Walton. The Prince's close connection with musical organisations led him to select no fewer than three choirs and three orchestras to perform these works, and there was a particularly fitting touch when the Maori soprano singer, Kiri Te Kanawa, was chosen to sing an aria from Handel's oratorio 'Samson' during the signing of the register. In addition, Sir David Willcocks was asked to compose a special arrangement of the National Anthem which would bring the service to its close.

The question which most frequently arises at the onset of a royal wedding is whether the bride will promise to obey her husband. Both the Queen and Princess Anne, for instance, undertook to obey theirs, but Lady Diana's vows did not include that promise: love, comfort, honour and keep she would, but obey she would not. The form of service used was the 1928

Alternative Series version, and this did in fact permit the omission of the promise of obedience. Lady Diana's decision was hailed as particularly apt in what was in theory at least an increasingly egalitarian institution.

By the end of March, the Privy Council had given its consent to the forthcoming marriage, and the Prince and his fiancée were, for the first time, photographed with the Queen – though not, it was noticed with some concern, with Prince Philip. Eventually, the Queen issued her authority for the preparation of a special Licence for the marriage to be solemnized, but by then

Before the royal processions left Buckingham Palace, the Society of Toastmasters executed one of their habitual functions on special public occasions. Repeating their gesture of goodwill to the Queen Mother on her 80th birthday the previous August, they held a public toast to the bride and groom outside the Palace Gates (3). Then it was all eyes – and all lenses (4) – on the Palace for those around the Queen Victoria Memorial. Eventually, the royal carriages began to file out: last to leave, before the bridegroom, were the Queen and Prince Philip (1) in a landau drawn by two bay horses. Then, to a royal salute, came the Prince of Wales (2) riding with his brother and chief supporter, Prince Andrew (5) in the 1902 State Landau. As they passed in front of the Palace railings (6), the groom was now irrevocably on his way to his wedding.

1

2

3

4

The activity of the early morning of the wedding day, which dawned bright and warm, alerted the waiting crowds to the business of the day. The areas of lawn and parkland around Buckingham Palace had long since been filled almost to capacity with groups and families sporting every type of red, white and blue clothing, as they watched the foot guards march out of (1 and 5) or past (2) the Palace towards their positions on the route. St James's Park (3) which had been almost a camp-site the night before, was now alive with colour, enriched by the crown-topped flagpoles and the copious flower baskets. At 10 am the Heads of the Armed Forces left the Palace (6) to inspect their men along the route, and shortly afterwards the royal procession began its long journey to St Paul's Cathedral. Princess Anne and Captain Mark Phillips rode with Princess Margaret and her son, Viscount Linley (4), while the Duke and Duchess of Gloucester rode with their son, the Earl of Ulster, and his grandmother, Princess Alice (7). Prince and Princess Michael of Kent travelled with members of the Queen's Household.

6

7

8

5

two somewhat untoward incidents began to ruffle the hitherto smooth passage of the wedding arrangements.

The first was the posting, early in May, of a letter bomb addressed to the Prince at Buckingham Palace. As it happened, he was at Balmoral at the time, and in any event an alert postal worker spotted and intercepted the package at the West Central sorting office. Although it was thought to be 'viable' at the time – designed, it seemed, to maim rather than to kill – it was later discovered to be a hoax device, sent by a middle-aged Zen Buddhist as part of a crusade against the evils of money. The details of his future campaign turned out, in the course of his trial in July, to be grisly indeed, and only heightened fears for the safety of royalty, guests and public on the wedding day.

These fears had already been set up by three recent major assassination alarms throughout the world – the attempts on the lives of President Reagan in March, and the Pope in May, and the almost unprecedented incident in London when a youth fired six blank shots at the Queen as she rode by on her way to the Trooping the Colour ceremony in mid-June. It suddenly seemed that even the operation involving three thousand police on the wedding day itself might be insufficient. As it was, the owners of every building which looked onto the processional route were required to forward to the police the names of all those who would be occupying their rooms and offices for the occasion, and a search was made of each building. In addition, the increasingly dangerous implications of the hunger strike campaign in Northern Ireland, which had already accounted for the lives of several IRA prisoners in the H-blocks of the Maze prison, made it necessary for constant security checks to be made at all ports and airports against the entry of known or suspected terrorists.

The second incident was of a less dangerous but more squalid nature. In March, Prince Charles had – publicly for the first time – kissed his tearful fiancée goodbye as he left Heathrow for a three-week tour of Australia and New Zealand. The tour itself was not without its difficulties for the Prince: there were demonstrations here and there against the monarchy, or the expense of the tour, or the possibility that Prince Charles might become Governor-General of Australia; and there was the usual crop of publicity stunts – bikini-clad girls rushing up to kiss him as he tried to take a morning dip in the sea off Bondi Beach, and a much more topical prank in which he came face-to-face with half a dozen young ladies dressed and coiffeured in the style of his bride-to-be: 'a put-up job,' he decided, rather scornfully.

But the most sinister episode came to light within hours of the Prince's return to Britain. During a short respite from official duties in Australia, he had stayed at the private residence of Mr Sinclair Hill, a trainer of polo ponies. Mr Hill had gone to the trouble of installing in his house a private telephone for the sole use of Prince Charles who needed to keep in touch with his family and fiancée back home. Despite the precaution of by-passing the national tele-communications network, it was claimed that some of the Prince's conversations with the Queen and Lady Diana had been surreptitiously recorded on tape. In addition to the obviously very personal nature of the calls, the revelation of which would understandably cause dismay, the Prince was alleged to have passed on some embarrassingly unflattering references about Mr Malcolm Fraser, the Prime Minister of Australia, whom he had necessarily met several times during his visit.

Tapes had been acquired by a freelance journalist, Simon Regan, the author some years previously of the book 'Charles, the Clown Prince', and he eventually sold the rights to his article based on the transcripts of the tapes to the German weekly magazine *Die Aktuelle*. The news caused great distress to Prince Charles and Lady Diana, who were trying to enjoy a short break together at Balmoral before resuming their duties, as well as immediate and feverish activity between the Palace and its lawyers, Farrer & Co. Believing then that the tapes might be genuine, and on the failure of diplomatic moves to discourage the imminent publication of the article, the Prince and Lady Diana obtained an injunction in Nuremberg on the very eve of publication. The editor had anticipated the prohibition however: printing was deliberately commenced earlier than usual, and by the time the injunction was legally served, several thousand copies had been printed and were in the course of distribution – thus effectively nullifying the injunction.

Almost a million copies were produced – about half as many again as normal – and although the British Government prohibited the entry of copies of the magazine into the United Kingdom, a few versions of the article did appear in Northern Ireland, Scotland and Northern England by way of an Irish newspaper which had secured the right to reproduce parts of it in Eire. By then, however, the Palace had been able to study the entire contents of the tapes and to establish that they were not genuine. A week later it was revealed, after a three-week investigation by Australian police and federal Intercom officials, that none of the telephone conversations could have been bugged and that it would

The royal wedding parade began in earnest with the march, past Buckingham Palace, of the last detachment of foot soldiers (2) and the placing of the final unit of massed bands along the route (5). The mounted guards (3 and 4), drawn from divisions of the Sovereign's Escort indicated that the processions were ready. Then, after the carriages bearing various members of the Kent and Gloucester families, the Phillipses and the Snowdons, came the Queen Mother's landau and the Queen and Prince Philip's carriage. Finally, Prince Charles emerged from the inner courtyard of the Palace (6) to embark upon the two-mile drive (1) to St Paul's.

5

6

have been totally impossible to monitor the Prince's calls.

It was shortly afterwards, at the end of May, that some 2,700 wedding invitations were formally issued from Buckingham Palace, and most were, predictably, accepted. Topping the entire list were, of course, members of the British Royal Family, and, for the first time in fourteen years it included the Earl of Harewood. The elder son of the late Princess Royal, and thus first cousin to the Queen, the Earl had been divorced in 1967 from his first wife (now Mrs Jeremy Thorpe) to marry Patricia Tuckwell by whom he had already had a child. Although his second marriage received formal royal consent, the ensuing rift between the Harewoods and the rest of the family precluded their presence at the funeral of the Duke of Windsor in 1972 and the wedding of Princess Anne the following year.

There was a last minute uncertainty when, a week before the wedding, the Queen Mother was ordered to rest after an ulcer on her shin, which she knocked when at Royal Ascot in June, developed an infection. By the weekend however, she was up and about again, and on the brink of her 81st birthday was able to be present, as

At 10.35 am the flat-topped Glass Coach, built for Queen Alexandra in 1910, carried Lady Diana from Clarence House, where she had been resident since her engagement, towards St Paul's. With her was her father, the eighth Earl Spencer. The bride was the last to leave, and by the time she had reached Ludgate Hill (1) most of the earlier procession had ended at the Cathedral. Only five minutes ahead of her was Prince Charles, who was thus the first to see London's own proclamation of goodwill as his mounted escort passed over Ludgate Circus (2). Just ahead of the bridegroom was the main procession which included, in one carriage, Princess Alexandra of Kent, her husband, Angus Ogilvy, and their children, James and Marina (3); in a following landau were the Duke and Duchess of Kent with two of their children, George, Earl of St Andrew's, and Lady Helen Windsor (4). Their other child, 11-year-old Lord Nicholas Windsor, acted as one of the two pages.

1

the widow of the last King of England, at the wedding of the next.

It seemed appropriate that the British Royal Family should be as fully represented as possible in view of the fact that kings and princes from eight ruling royal families in Europe would be present, as well as those from four former monarchies, and from the more distant thrones of Japan, Nepal, Thailand, Swaziland, Tonga and Samoa. The only notable absentees in this respect were the King and Queen of Spain who opted out ten days before the wedding when it was revealed that the perfectly legitimate but, in the circumstances, somewhat insensitive decision had been taken to send the Royal Yacht *Britannia* to the Rock of Gibraltar – owned by Britain but claimed by Spain – for the start of the foreign leg of the royal honeymoon.

2

3

The congregation was further swelled by over two dozen Commonwealth heads of state, five European presidents, including the newly elected President Mitterand of France, and Mrs Nancy Reagan, the 'happy, flattered and excited' wife of the American President. In her case there was an amusing and minor difficulty of protocol, arising over the question of whether she should curtsey when being presented to the Queen. It arose out of a previous furore during the visit of the Prince of Wales to the United States in April, when the wife of a former Ambassador to Britain greeted him with a deferentially low curtsey. The storm of outrage and opprobrium was as fierce as it was sudden, and came from a contingent of strongly patriotic American ladies. 'How dare she,' wrote one in the full spate of her anger, 'representing this great, free country, being the first to greet a figurehead prince from

1

2

3

4

another country, bend her knees in obeisance as a serf of yore?' 'We do not,' added another, 'bend the knee in this country before any except God. I would hope that our officials could manage to greet visitors, of whatever rank, with courtesy and in a dignified and upright position.' And so it went on, with an unjustifiably heated debate, in the absence of an established procedure, as to the correct form of greeting foreign royalty. Mrs Reagan later learned, no doubt with considerable relief, that a mere handshake would be sufficient for her visit to England.

A sizeable proportion of the wedding guests consisted of representatives of the many organisations with which Prince Charles is officially connected, but it was pleasant, rather typical, and wholly appropriate in the 'private' context of the occasion, to find people in St Paul's whose connection with the royal couple was of a very personal nature. These included teachers from Lady Diana's kindergarten, two members of the old team from The Goon Show – a particular favourite of Prince Charles in the 1950's and early 1960's – and a Bahamian couple who, during his private visit to

The Queen's carriage, with the Queen and Duke of Edinburgh acknowledging the greetings of their people (4), heads up Ludgate Hill towards the Cathedral. Behind them is Prince Charles' landau. The splendid spectacle of mounted guards in formation is shown (3) as an Escort of the Household Brigades follows the carriage taking Princess Alexandra and her family to St Paul's. As the Queen arrives there, she and her mother turn to give a last wave (6) before entering the West door for the service. Meanwhile, the two youngest bridesmaids have been ushered in by chief bridesmaid, Lady Sarah Armstrong-Jones (9). She is later responsible, with India Hicks, for adjusting Lady Diana's train as she arrives at the Cathedral – though the bride still has to turn as she mounts the steps to make sure that all is in order (7). Finally, on the arm of her father, who despite his recent severe and debilitating illness was determined to take his youngest daughter to the altar, Lady Diana begins her slow measured walk (5) to where Prince Charles awaits her. Her full, 25-feet long train stretches out behind her (8) as she makes her way up the nave, followed by the beautifully dressed bridesmaids with their garlands of summer flowers, and the smartly turned-out pages, all of whom set off the magnificence of the bride's voluminous ivory silk dress. The full complement of the bride's assistants is seen (1) in the Cathedral: (left to right) Lady Sarah Armstrong-Jones, Edward van Cutsem, Lord Nicholas Windsor, Sarah Gaselee, India Hicks, Clementine Hambro and Catherine Cameron.

Eleuthera some years before as the guest of Countess Mountbatten, had kept house for him.

By June, the preparations for what was already known as 'The Wedding of the Century' were in their final stages, and the souvenir trade in particular was in full cry. Early in April the Lord Chamberlain had discharged another of his many functions by defining the acceptable and unacceptable forms in which producers of souvenirs might commemorate the great day. Scarves and beer mugs were in, as were plastic carrier bags: paper carrier bags were not approved owing to their lack of permanence. Tea towels and rugs were not favoured either, it being considered inappropriate that the royal likenesses should be wiped around wet crockery or walked upon. T-shirts were also ruled out – a decision which drew the contempt of the Association of Textile Manufacturers, who recommended its members to ignore it, though still to observe the standards of good taste. One Irish linen firm cleverly anticipated both the engagement and any restriction imposed by Lord Maclean by producing tea towels well

5

6   7

Slowly, and to the tune of the Prince of Denmark's March, Lady Diana is led along the 500 foot red carpet towards the waiting clergy (2). After some three minutes, she reaches the point where Prince Charles, Prince Andrew and Prince Edward stand, ready for her arrival (5). They all move forward to face the Dean of St Paul's, the Very Reverend Alan Webster, who introduces the marriage ceremony to the congregation (3). Following this, the Archbishop of Canterbury,

Dr Robert Runcie, conducts the service of solemnisation, then leads the bride and groom forward to the Sicilian marbled High Altar while the choir sing Parry's Anthem 'I was glad' (6). Finally, towards the end of the service, the newly-married couple kneel in prayer before the Archbishop (7). The photograph opposite (1) vividly depicts the architectural splendour of St Paul's and the richness and colour of its traditional ritual.

1

3

4

2

5

in advance of 24th February for sale within five minutes of the announcement of the engagement.

By the time the wedding took place, the country was awash with souvenirs of every conceivable kind, and for as much or as little as the consumer could wish to pay. From the cheapest crockery at less than £1, there were offerings of bone china plates with 22-carat gold-plate trimmings for £35, silver pill-boxes for £40, silver spoons at £275 per set of six, a sterling silver and gold tankard and plate set for £396, barometers from Garrards at £575, and 9-carat gold goblets for a mere £1,800. Philatelists had a field day, with the opportunity to buy complete sets of Commonwealth first day covers from 40 countries for £158, and collectors of medals and medallions could pay the Birmingham Mint £4.45 for a bronze commemorative medal or £598 for a 22-carat gold one.

The souvenir bonanza was given official blessing of a sort when a Design Centre panel, headed by Princess Margaret's former husband Lord Snowdon, approved a selection of souvenirs which included the much maligned T-shirt, a tea-cosy, a play-ball designed like an orb, and a baby's rattle in the shape of a royal sceptre. One of the best selling articles, also favoured by the Design Centre, was a mug or loving cup showing a caricature of Prince Charles on the front, and copious handles representing his ears. We may know in time what the Prince thought about that one!

Almost as if to keep potential criticism by Mr Willie Hamilton and his supporters out of the headlines, the projected costs of the wedding preparations did not feature too strongly in the now daily gobbets of news being released on the subject. There were, however, a few clues: £50,000 was being spent by the Department of the Environment for flowers to decorate the full length of the Mall, and for the red carpet which would cover the aisle of St Paul's Cathedral. A further £80,000 would cover the cost of some two tons of explosives which would fill over 12,000 fireworks for a mammoth display in Hyde Park – though these costs were to be defrayed by charges to the BBC and ITV for televising the event, and any profits would go to a fund for the Year of the Disabled. The display took place on the eve of the wedding, before an estimated crowd of over half a million people, and was reckoned to be the biggest of its kind in this country since the famous Royal Fireworks of 1749, for which Handel wrote the music of the same name. On this occasion, too, there was music in abundance, provided by several civil and military massed bands and choirs. The Prince of Wales lit the first of 101 bonfires which carried the commemorative message from beacon to beacon throughout the country, in the manner of those which celebrated the Queen's Silver Jubilee in 1977.

The Archbishop gives his blessing on the Prince and Princess of Wales (4) and, after the signing of the Register, the couple take their first steps together as man and wife (2). Then comes the sedate walk down the long red carpet (1) and out onto the summit of the grand flight of steps at the West door, where the Princess waves joyfully to an equally joyful people (6). Finally, they (5) and the Queen and Earl Spencer (3) settle into their carriages for the return to the Palace.

Those who cared to calculate the value of 170 lbs of fruit, nuts, sugar, butter, eggs and several other ingredients of the royal wedding cake would probably come nowhere near its true cost without knowledge of the total number of man-hours required to prepare and bake it. This job was done by the Royal Naval Cookery School aboard HMS Pembroke at Chatham, under the direction of Chief Petty Officer Cook, David Avery. The cake weighed around 1½ cwt, stood four feet high and contained about 150 eggs. Four people spent six hours each cleaning and sorting over 100 lbs of dried fruit, and a further four worked on the mixing with electric beaters before the entire cake spent nine hours in the ship's oven.

Other outward and official signs of the forthcoming event were quickly coming to the fore. Following the tradition set by the Royal Mint during celebrations for the Queen's Silver Wedding in 1972, her Silver Jubilee and the Queen Mother's eightieth birthday, a crown piece was produced in July, bearing the portraits of Prince Charles and his bride. The standard cupro-nickel

coin cost its face value of 25 pence, whilst a sterling silver issue was marketed at over £28. As usual, local authorities in many parts of the country distributed gifts of crowns (cupro-nickel version) to local schoolchildren but in Porthmadog a local solicitor's offer to provide 300 crowns for the purpose was blocked by a fervent Welsh nationalist school governor. Additional bad grace came from the new Labour leader of the GLC, Mr Ken Livingstone, who deriding the prospect as a type of 'self inflicted torture', declared that none of the Council officials should attend the wedding. It was pointed out

The reception given to the bride and groom on their journey back from St Paul's Cathedral was more ear-splitting than anyone could have imagined. From the moment when that first great roar went up it was clear that the new Princess would be the darling of

the vast crowds. And so it proved to be–as the couple quitted the precincts of the Cathedral (4), leaving the deafening cheers behind them, they came upon another burst of acclamation at Ludgate Circus (2), and their ride down the Strand (1) was

tumultuous. Through it all, the Princess responded modestly but with evident delight. There were renewed cheers for the Queen, who left accompanied by Earl Spencer (3) and for Prince Philip who escorted the bride's mother to the Palace (5).

1

2

4

5

The Prince and Princess of Wales returned to Buckingham Palace (2), but their obligations to their public were not yet over. Though balcony appearances after occasions such as this are now almost standard, there is no procedural inevitability that the family will appear. However, the awning on the balcony fascia was sufficient to assure the eager crowds that they would have the chance to see their new Princess. It was not long before the couple came onto the balcony to receive the congratulations of those below (1). They were soon joined by their pages, Edward van Cutsem and Lord Nicholas Windsor (3), and by the Queen and the younger bridesmaids (4, 5 and 6). Ultimately the entire immediate families of both bride and groom came out to see the massive crowd which was being swelled by more

and more people surging down the Mall towards the Palace. The full balcony scene (7) includes (left to right) Lord Spencer, Ruth Lady Fermoy (the bride's grandmother) the Duke of Edinburgh, Queen Elizabeth the Queen Mother, Lord Nicholas Windsor, Edward van Cutsem, Sarah Gaselee, Catherine Cameron, the Princess of Wales. Clementine Hambro, the Prince of Wales, the Queen, Prince Edward, Mrs Shand-Kydd, and Prince Andrew. Even this army of royals did not satisfy the demand of the crowds. They called the bride and groom back several times and in all there were four separate appearances – almost a record for encores! It was only when the tall balcony window-doors were closed that the crowd realised that it would see no more until the couple left for their honeymoon, and began to make its way back to the shops or royal parks for lunch.

that insofar as invitations had been sent out to the Chairman and Director-General of the GLC, Mr Livingstone would have no right to proscribe their acceptance. But, despite the hopes of several Councillors that representatives should be permitted to go to the wedding, a vote decided that invitations should be refused and allotted to someone 'happier in that sort of setting.'

In the meantime the people of Clay Cross, a parish of earlier political fame in North Derbyshire, found themselves at odds over the decision by the local council to hold a Republican Day celebration on 29th July, instead of any events to mark the royal wedding. The celebrations would involve the hiring of a local theatre group who would depict 'the other side of the monarchy' – in the words of the leader of the council, Mr Clifford Fox. 'We hope,' he added, 'that they will show how the monarchy affects us all, and its effects on the working class people and…what it actually costs us.' There were pained protests from local royalists about the council's attempts to 'turn the parish into a Communist state' and, more seriously, threats of violence, and damage to the local community centre where the republican junketings were to be held. Ultimately the event was virtually called off.

Meanwhile, a Manchester firm of blast cleaners decided to clean Hartshead Pike, a now blackened monument on the Lancashire moors which had been erected to commemorate the wedding of the last Prince of Wales to be married as such – the future King Edward VII – in 1863. Down in Essex there was, on the contrary, bitter criticism of the County Council's plan to spend £600 on photographs of Prince Charles and Lady Diana to be put up in schools, libraries and old peoples' homes throughout the County. The Post Office introduced a pair of new commemorative stamps, each bearing the portrait of the couple by Lord Snowdon: the advance publicity of this issue prompted one sceptical press cartoonist to express surprise at the fact that the Post Office, never particularly renowned for its ability to hold down prices, could commit itself to maintaining the price of first class postage for the whole of the six weeks between then and the wedding! London Transport's contribution to the event was the issue of a ticket offering unlimited travel on the wedding day on almost all London buses and tubes: for the price of £2 (60p for children) there was a ticket showing pictures of the bride and groom, photographs of Buckingham Palace and St Paul's, and a map of the processional route.

The BBC and ITV in due course announced their plans for the transmission of the wedding ceremony, which, it was estimated, would be beamed to over 500 million people in Europe and throughout the world. Programmes started as early as 7.30 in the morning, with a visit by ITV to the stables at Chelsea Barracks where the horses were being groomed and saddled up: there were on-the-spot reports from royal residences and places of royal association such as Caernarvon Castle, interviews with units of the armed forces, guided tours of HMS *Bronington,* quests for dressmakers, cooks, broadcasters and anyone else who had ever had connections with previous royal occasions, and endless interviews with countless 'men in the street' for their views on this wedding and their reminiscences of previous ones.

Throughout all this, Prince Charles and Lady Diana continued with their round of duties until the last of their official engagements, a visit to battalions of the Cheshire Regiment at Tidworth in Hampshire. This was the end of what for Lady Diana had been something of a crash course in the art and science of being royal and observing some of the time-honoured protocol requirements of that status. She had indeed attended a varied selection of functions, from Royal Ascot to the State Banquet given in London by the visiting King Khalid of Saudi-Arabia, and from the Trooping the Colour and Garter ceremonies to a delightfully informal visit to Broadlands, the home of the Mountbatten family where she and Prince Charles would spend the first part of their honeymoon. During this engagement – and indeed in the course of several other visits to towns and villages further west – Lady Diana gave more than a hint of an approach to royal duties which looked fresher and more innovative than any style adopted by her future in-laws. Few of them had ever picked up other people's babies, pulled caps over children's faces, allowed their hands to be kissed by adventurous schoolboys or shown their engagement rings off to the crowds but here, suddenly, was someone who did – and a future Princess of Wales at that.

It remains to be seen how far this distinctly novel approach flourishes after the Princess of Wales – or Princess' Charles, if she ever becomes known by that quaint title – settles down as a fully-fledged member of the busy royal firm. It seems to work well, and if that is the case, it should do well. If that happens we may well see a corresponding change in Prince Charles' own style, which though adaptable and flexible to an extent, has been somewhat conservative in the past. This will be no untoward development, since, with the prospect of many years remaining of his long apprenticeship for the Throne, the pitfall of staleness and stagnation would be fatal. The new Princess' youth and modest flair brings with it a promise that the impact of a considerably younger generation is about to be felt in the royal midst. There could be no doubt that, as she and her husband left St Paul's Cathedral on 29th July, they were surrounded by the loyalty of the vast proportion of their future

The wedding ceremony was witnessed by representatives from all the reigning royal families of Europe except Spain, whose King Juan Carlos stayed away because the foreign part of the honeymoon was to begin at Gibraltar. With the Prince and Princess of Wales (5) and their pages and bridesmaids are (left to right) King Carl of Sweden, Prince Henrik of Denmark, Queen Silvia of Sweden, Queen Margrethe of Denmark, King Baudouin of Belgium, King Olav of Norway, James Ogilvy, Queen Fabiola of Belgium, Marina Ogilvy, Princess Margaret, Captain Mark Phillips, Princess Anne, Angus Ogilvy,

Princess Alexandra, the Queen Mother, Prince Andrew, Viscount Linley, the Duchess of Gloucester, Prince Philip, the Queen, the Duke of Gloucester, Prince Edward, Princess Alice of Gloucester, the Duke of Kent, Ruth Lady Fermoy, the Earl of St Andrew's, Mrs Shand-Kydd, the Duchess of Kent, Viscount Althorp, Lady Jane Fellowes, Earl Spencer, Anthony Fellowes, Prince Michael, Lady Sarah McCorquodale, Princess Michael, Neil McCorquodale, Queen Beatrix of the Netherlands, Princess Grace of Monaco, Prince Claus of the Netherlands, Prince Albert of Monaco, Lady Helen Windsor, Princess Gina of Liechtenstein, Grand Duke Jean of Luxembourg, Prince Franz-Josef of Liechtenstein, and Grand Duchess Josephine-Charlotte of Luxembourg. This photograph, like all on these pages, was taken by the Queen's cousin, Lord Lichfield. A smaller group (3) includes only the immediate families of the bride and groom. The formal portraits are very much in the traditional style: the Prince and Princesss with their supporters, pages and bridesmaids, make good use of the long train to form a well-balanced whole (2).

subjects, and by the fascinated interest of millions around the world. The Prince himself has done an enormous amount of work in the last decade or so to keep that interest and loyalty alive and relevant in circumstances where they might well have died away long ago. While our new Princess, for whom a new and daunting chapter in life now begins, will inevitably be called upon to adapt herself, she may equally well expect to be able to adapt others to the requirement of what she sees to be the monarchy of the future – one to which, having embarked upon it 'without any doubts at all', she is now fully committed.

It has been the most splendid day: a nerve-wracking, emotional day; a busy but happy day. Certainly an intensely public day. Now a welcome period of privacy was in sight for Prince Charles and his wife. Late in the afternoon they left Buckingham Palace (this page), hotly pursued by relatives and retainers with confetti, and in a carriage bedecked with balloons and a "Just Married" notice stuck on the back. They were to have a short stay at Broadlands – via

Waterloo Station and Romsey, then a few weeks on the Royal Yacht before returning to home soil. In less than a year, Lady Diana Spencer has captured more hearts than that of her Prince. After the rumours and speculation, the publicity and the harassment, she has emerged as a popular Princess of Wales and, as the picture opposite shows, as a serene and contented wife of a proud and fulfilled husband.

Producer: Ted Smart.
Editor: David Gibbon.
Designer: Philip Clucas, MSIAD.
Research Consultant: Trevor Hall.

© 1981 Illustrations and text:
Colour Library International Ltd.
New Malden, Surrey, England.

Colour separations by
FERCROM, Barcelona, Spain.
Display and text filmsetting by
The Printed Word and Focus Photoset,

London, England.

Printed by Cayfosa bound by Sagarra
y Marmol-Barcelona-Spain

First English edition published in 1981 by
Colour Library International Ltd.
This edition published by Beekman House
Distributed by Crown Publishers, Inc.
h g f e d c b a
All rights reserved.
ISBN 0-517- 367858

Library of Congress Catalogue Card No. 81-69936